The Vietnam War

American history, Volume 3

Michael Johnson

Published by Harmony House Publishing, 2024.

While every precaution has been taken in the preparation of this book, the publisher assumes no responsibility for errors or omissions, or for damages resulting from the use of the information contained herein.

THE VIETNAM WAR

First edition. March 23, 2024.

Copyright © 2024 Michael Johnson.

ISBN: 979-8224172405

Written by Michael Johnson.

Table of Contents

"To the brave souls who endured the trials of the Vietnam War, and to those whose lives were forever altered by its tumultuous legacy, this book is dedicated. Your courage, sacrifice, and resilience inspire us to strive for understanding, healing, and reconciliation in the face of adversity. May the lessons learned from this turbulent chapter in history guide us towards a future of peace, compassion, and unity."

Chapter 1: Introduction

Setting the stage: Historical background leading up to the Vietnam War

The Vietnam War was not an isolated event but rather a culmination of complex historical, political, and social factors that had been brewing for decades. To understand the origins and evolution of this conflict, it is essential to delve into the rich tapestry of history that shaped the course of events in Vietnam and the broader international context.

Vietnam, a nation steeped in a long tradition of resistance to foreign domination, had been under colonial rule for much of its modern history. In the 19th century, Vietnam, along with its neighbors Laos and Cambodia, was part of French Indochina, a colonial possession of the French Empire. French colonial rule brought about significant social, economic, and cultural changes in Vietnam, as well as resistance from the local population.

One of the key figures in Vietnam's struggle for independence was Ho Chi Minh, a Vietnamese communist revolutionary who would later become the leader of North Vietnam. Ho Chi Minh's political awakening was shaped by his experiences abroad, where he witnessed the injustices of colonialism and imperialism. Inspired by the ideals of Marxism-Leninism and the successful communist revolutions in Russia and China, Ho Chi Minh founded the Vietnamese Communist Party in 1930 and dedicated his life to the liberation of his homeland.

The Japanese occupation of Vietnam during World War II further fueled nationalist sentiments and resistance against foreign rule. While the Japanese overthrow of French colonial administration initially appeared as a step towards independence, it soon became evident that Japan sought to exploit Vietnam for its own strategic interests. Vietnamese resistance groups, including Ho Chi Minh's Viet Minh, waged guerrilla warfare against the Japanese occupiers and their collaborators, earning widespread support from the Vietnamese populace.

The end of World War II brought about seismic shifts in the global balance of power, with the defeat of Axis powers paving the way for the emergence of new superpowers: the United States and the Soviet Union. The onset of the Cold War, characterized by ideological rivalry, geopolitical maneuvering, and proxy conflicts, had profound implications for Vietnam and other formerly colonized nations seeking independence.

At the heart of the Cold War rivalry was the ideological struggle between capitalism and communism. The United States, as the leader of the capitalist bloc, viewed the spread of communism as a threat to its global interests and embarked on a policy of containment aimed at preventing the further expansion of Soviet influence. This policy manifested in various forms, including military intervention, covert operations, and economic aid to anti-communist regimes.

Meanwhile, in Vietnam, the struggle for independence entered a new phase as the French sought to reassert control over their former colony. The First Indochina War (1946-1954) pitted the French colonial forces against the Viet Minh in a protracted and bloody conflict. Despite initial French military successes, the Viet Minh, led by Ho Chi Minh, proved resilient and resourceful, drawing on popular support and waging a guerrilla campaign against the better-equipped French forces.

The turning point of the First Indochina War came in 1954 with the decisive Battle of Dien Bien Phu, where the Viet Minh successfully besieged and defeated the French garrison, leading to France's eventual withdrawal from Vietnam. The Geneva Conference of 1954, convened to negotiate a settlement to the conflict, resulted in the partition of Vietnam along the 17th parallel, with Ho Chi Minh's communist government controlling the north and a US-backed regime led by Ngo Dinh Diem governing the south.

Overview of key players and events that shaped the conflict

The Vietnam War, which officially began in 1955 and lasted until 1975, was not merely a civil war but a complex geopolitical struggle with far-reaching implications. At its core were the competing visions of the two Vietnams: the communist North, led by Ho Chi Minh and the National Liberation Front (NLF), and the anti-communist South, backed by the United States and its allies.

In the North, Ho Chi Minh emerged as a charismatic and resolute leader, revered by his followers as the father of Vietnamese independence. Under his leadership, North Vietnam received military and economic aid from the Soviet Union and China, enabling it to build a formidable army and pursue its goal of reunifying the country under communist rule.

Meanwhile, in South Vietnam, political instability and internal divisions plagued the US-backed government of Ngo Dinh Diem. Despite receiving substantial military and financial support from the United States, the Diem regime faced widespread opposition from communist insurgents, dissident factions, and disenfranchised peasants. Diem's authoritarian rule, marked by corruption, repression, and religious discrimination, alienated large segments of the population and fueled support for the communist insurgency.

The United States, under the leadership of President Dwight D. Eisenhower, initially adopted a policy of providing military aid and advisory support to the South Vietnamese government in its fight against communist insurgents. However, the escalating conflict and the perceived threat of communist expansion in Southeast Asia prompted the United States to deepen its involvement in Vietnam.

The election of President John F. Kennedy in 1960 brought a new sense of urgency to US policy in Vietnam. Kennedy's administration increased military assistance to South Vietnam and expanded covert operations against communist insurgents. The introduction of US military advisors and Special Forces units marked the beginning of direct American involvement in the conflict.

The Gulf of Tonkin Incident in August 1964 provided the pretext for further escalation, as President Lyndon B. Johnson secured congressional approval for the Gulf of Tonkin Resolution, granting him broad powers to wage war in Vietnam. The subsequent deployment of US combat troops marked a significant escalation of the conflict, as American forces became increasingly embroiled in a protracted and costly war against determined communist adversaries.

As the war dragged on, it became increasingly clear that military victory was elusive and that the conflict had profound social, political, and economic costs for both Vietnam and the United States. The Tet Offensive of 1968, a massive coordinated assault by communist forces on cities and military installations across South Vietnam, dealt a severe blow to American morale and public confidence in the war effort.

Despite massive US military firepower and technological superiority, the North Vietnamese and Viet Cong guerrillas proved resilient and adaptable, inflicting heavy casualties on American forces and eroding public support for the war at home. Growing anti-war protests, draft resistance, and dissent within the military further undermined the Johnson and subsequent Nixon administrations' efforts to sustain public backing for the war.

The Vietnam War was not only a military conflict but also a moral and ideological struggle that divided American society and challenged the nation's self-image as a force for freedom and democracy. The war's legacy continues to shape American foreign policy, military doctrine, and public discourse on war and peace, serving as a cautionary tale of the perils of interventionism and the limits of military power in achieving political objectives.

Chapter 2: Roots of Conflict

Exploration of colonial history and the rise of Vietnamese nationalism

Vietnam's journey toward independence was deeply intertwined with its colonial past and the emergence of nationalist movements seeking to liberate the country from foreign domination. The seeds of Vietnamese nationalism were sown during the era of French colonial rule, as the Vietnamese people grappled with the challenges of modernization, exploitation, and cultural assimilation.

The French colonization of Vietnam began in the mid-19th century, following the decline of the ruling Nguyen dynasty and the imposition of unequal treaties that ceded control of Vietnamese territory to France. Under the pretext of civilizing the "barbaric" natives and spreading the blessings of Western civilization, the French embarked on a project of colonial conquest and exploitation that would shape the destiny of Vietnam for generations to come.

Central to the French colonial enterprise was the exploitation of Vietnam's natural resources, labor force, and strategic geographical position. The French imposed a system of land tenure that favored large landowners and French colonial elites at the expense of Vietnamese peasants, who were forced to toil on plantations and rubber estates owned by foreign corporations. The introduction of cash crops such as rubber, coffee, and tea further disrupted traditional agrarian economies and exacerbated social inequalities.

The French also sought to impose their cultural, linguistic, and religious values on the Vietnamese population, viewing them as inferior and in need of "civilizing" through Western education and Christianization. French missionaries and educators established schools, churches, and institutions aimed at indoctrinating Vietnamese youth with French language, culture, and ideals of loyalty to the colonial authorities.

However, the French colonial project faced fierce resistance from the Vietnamese people, who refused to accept their subjugation and actively sought ways to assert their national identity and reclaim their sovereignty. One of the earliest expressions of Vietnamese nationalism was the Can Vuong movement, led by the scholar-activist Phan Dinh Phung, which sought to mobilize popular support for resistance against French encroachment.

The Can Vuong movement was followed by the rise of modern nationalist organizations such as the Dong Du movement, founded by Phan Boi Chau, which advocated for political reforms, social justice, and national independence. Drawing inspiration from anti-colonial movements in Asia and Africa, Vietnamese nationalists sought to forge alliances with like-minded activists and intellectuals across the globe, including in China, Japan, and Europe.

The turning point in Vietnam's struggle for independence came with the emergence of the Vietnamese Communist Party (VCP), founded in 1930 by revolutionary leader Ho Chi Minh. Inspired by the ideals of Marxism-Leninism and the success of the Bolshevik Revolution in Russia, Ho Chi Minh and his comrades envisioned a Vietnam free from colonial oppression and exploitation, where the working class would seize power and build a socialist society.

The VCP, later renamed the Indochinese Communist Party (ICP), played a pivotal role in organizing resistance against French colonial rule and mobilizing the masses in support of national liberation. Through its armed wing, the Viet Minh (Vietnamese Independence League), the ICP waged guerrilla warfare against French colonial forces and collaborated with nationalist and anti-colonial movements across Southeast Asia.

Examination of the role of French colonization

and the First Indochina War

The French colonization of Vietnam, Laos, and Cambodia, collectively known as French Indochina, laid the groundwork for the protracted conflict that would engulf the region in the decades to come. French colonial rule was characterized by exploitation, repression, and cultural assimilation, as well as resistance from the indigenous populations seeking to reclaim their sovereignty.

The French conquest of Vietnam began in the 1850s with the establishment of colonial outposts in Cochinchina (Southern Vietnam) and Tonkin (Northern Vietnam), followed by the annexation of Annam (Central Vietnam) and the establishment of the protectorate of Tonkin. French control over Vietnam was solidified through a combination of military conquest, diplomatic maneuvering, and collaboration with local elites.

The colonial administration imposed a system of direct rule, with French governors-general overseeing the administration of Vietnamese territories and implementing policies aimed at extracting resources, maximizing profits, and maintaining social order. French officials and settlers occupied key positions in the colonial bureaucracy, economy, and society, while indigenous Vietnamese were relegated to subordinate roles and denied basic rights and freedoms.

One of the most significant legacies of French colonial rule in Vietnam was the transformation of the economy from subsistence agriculture to a cash-crop export economy geared toward serving the needs of the colonial metropole. Vietnamese peasants were forced off their lands and compelled to work as wage laborers on French-owned plantations and mines, producing commodities such as rice, rubber, and coal for export to the global market.

The exploitation of Vietnam's natural resources and labor force fueled discontent and resistance among the Vietnamese population, leading to periodic outbreaks of peasant uprisings, anti-colonial protests, and acts of sabotage against French colonial authorities and collaborators. The French responded with repressive measures, including martial law, censorship, and mass arrests, in an attempt to quell dissent and maintain control over the colony.

Despite the formidable power of the French colonial state, resistance to French rule persisted and intensified over time, fueled by nationalist sentiments, socio-economic grievances, and the spread of revolutionary ideas from abroad. The emergence of nationalist organizations such as the Vietnamese Nationalist Party (VNQDD) and the Indochinese Communist Party (ICP) provided a rallying point for anti-colonial activists and intellectuals seeking to overthrow French rule and establish an independent Vietnam.

The outbreak of World War II and the subsequent Japanese occupation of Vietnam presented both challenges and opportunities for the Vietnamese nationalist movement. While the Japanese occupation regime imposed harsh measures and exploited Vietnamese resources for its war effort, it also weakened French colonial control and created space for nationalist resistance and mobilization.

The First Indochina War (1946-1954), also known as the Anti-French Resistance War, marked the culmination of decades of struggle against French colonial rule and the beginning of Vietnam's quest for independence. The war was sparked by a series of incidents, including clashes between French and Viet Minh forces, as well as the refusal of the French colonial authorities to grant Vietnam full autonomy and self-government.

The Viet Minh, under the leadership of Ho Chi Minh, emerged as the vanguard of the anti-colonial struggle, mobilizing peasants, workers, and intellectuals in a protracted guerrilla war against French colonial forces. Despite being outnumbered and outgunned, the Viet Minh employed innovative tactics, including hit-and-run attacks, ambushes, and underground resistance networks, to harass and weaken the French colonial garrisons.

The turning point of the First Indochina War came with the Battle of Dien Bien Phu in 1954, where the Viet Minh launched a surprise assault on a heavily fortified French garrison in the remote highlands of northwest Vietnam. After a grueling 56-day siege, the Viet Minh succeeded in overrunning the French positions and inflicting heavy casualties, forcing the French to negotiate a settlement to the conflict.

The Geneva Accords of 1954, signed by France, Vietnam, Laos, Cambodia, the Soviet Union, the United States, and China, formally ended the First Indochina War and laid the groundwork for the partition of Vietnam along the 17th parallel. While the accords called for nationwide elections to reunify Vietnam under a single government, they also created separate temporary military demarcation zones in the north and south, pending the outcome of the elections.

The French withdrawal from Vietnam following the Geneva Accords marked the end of direct French colonial rule but did not bring about a lasting peace or reconciliation between North and South Vietnam. Instead, the partition of Vietnam into two separate entities, with the communist government in the North and the US-backed regime in the South, set the stage for further conflict and division.

In the North, the Democratic Republic of Vietnam (DRV), led by Ho Chi Minh and the Viet Minh, consolidated its control over the newly liberated territories and embarked on a program of nation-building, economic reconstruction, and social reform. Ho Chi Minh's government implemented land reforms, collectivization of agriculture, and industrialization policies aimed at modernizing the economy and consolidating its political power.

Meanwhile, in the South, the Republic of Vietnam (RVN), led by Ngo Dinh Diem, faced numerous challenges, including political instability, economic stagnation, and internal divisions. Diem's authoritarian rule, characterized by nepotism, corruption, and repression of political dissent, alienated large segments of the population and fueled support for communist insurgents and opposition movements.

The division of Vietnam along ideological lines, with the North aligned with the communist bloc led by the Soviet Union and China, and the South aligned with the Western powers led by the United States, set the stage for a new phase of conflict and confrontation. The United States, viewing Vietnam as a crucial battleground in the global struggle against communism, began to increase its military and economic aid to the South Vietnamese government, as well as deploy military advisors and personnel to assist in the fight against communist insurgents.

The period following the Geneva Accords was marked by escalating tensions and sporadic outbreaks of violence along the demilitarized zone (DMZ) separating North and South Vietnam. Both sides engaged in covert operations, sabotage, and propaganda campaigns aimed at undermining the other's legitimacy and consolidating their own power. The Cold War rivalry between the United States and the Soviet Union intensified, with Vietnam becoming a focal point of their strategic competition for influence in Southeast Asia.

The simmering conflict in Vietnam erupted into full-scale war in 1959 with the outbreak of the Second Indochina War, commonly known as the Vietnam War. The war, which lasted for over two decades, was characterized by massive military mobilization, aerial bombardment, chemical warfare, and brutal guerrilla fighting, resulting in widespread devastation, suffering, and loss of life on all sides.

The roots of the Vietnam War can be traced back to the unresolved contradictions and legacies of colonialism, imperialism, and nationalism that had shaped Vietnam's history for centuries. The French colonization of Vietnam, with its legacy of exploitation, repression, and cultural assimilation, sowed the seeds of resistance and rebellion that would eventually blossom into a full-blown revolution against foreign rule.

The First Indochina War, fought between the Viet Minh and the French colonial forces, laid the groundwork for the subsequent conflict by weakening French control and emboldening Vietnamese nationalists to pursue their aspirations for independence. The victory of the Viet

Minh at Dien Bien Phu and the subsequent Geneva Accords signaled the end of French colonial rule but also created the conditions for further conflict and division between North and South Vietnam.

The Vietnam War, with its complex web of political, economic, and ideological factors, defies simple explanations or easy solutions. It was not merely a struggle for national liberation or ideological supremacy but a multifaceted conflict driven by competing interests, historical grievances, and geopolitical ambitions. The roots of the Vietnam War run deep, reflecting the enduring legacy of colonialism and imperialism in shaping the destinies of nations and peoples across the globe.

Chapter 3: American Involvement Begins

Analysis of American support for France in Indochina

The United States' involvement in Vietnam can be traced back to its support for France during the First Indochina War, a conflict between the French colonial authorities and the Viet Minh, the communist-led nationalist movement fighting for Vietnamese independence. American assistance to France in its efforts to retain control over its colonial possessions in Southeast Asia laid the groundwork for deeper American involvement in Vietnam in the years to come.

In the aftermath of World War II, the United States emerged as a global superpower, committed to containing the spread of communism and promoting the interests of the Western capitalist bloc. As part of this broader strategy, the United States viewed Southeast Asia, and Vietnam in particular, as a critical battleground in the Cold War struggle against communist expansionism.

American policymakers feared that the loss of Vietnam to communism would not only jeopardize US strategic interests in the region but also embolden communist movements in other parts of Asia and beyond. Therefore, when France requested American military and economic assistance in its efforts to reassert control over Vietnam, the United States was quick to respond.

The Truman administration, followed by the Eisenhower administration, provided France with substantial financial aid, military equipment, and logistical support to bolster its colonial war effort in Vietnam. The United States saw France as a key ally in Europe and Asia and was willing to support its efforts to maintain control over its colonies, even at the risk of exacerbating tensions with the Soviet Union and China.

American support for France in Indochina took various forms, including military advisors, economic aid, and diplomatic backing. American military advisors were sent to Vietnam to train French colonial troops and provide technical assistance in counterinsurgency operations against the Viet Minh guerrillas. American economic aid helped finance France's war effort and alleviate the financial burden of maintaining its colonial empire in Southeast Asia.

Diplomatically, the United States lobbied for international support for France's position in Vietnam and sought to isolate the Viet Minh diplomatically by portraying them as agents of international communism and subversion. The United States also played a key role in organizing the Southeast Asia Treaty Organization (SEATO), a regional alliance aimed at containing communist aggression in Southeast Asia and providing collective defense against external threats.

Despite American support, France's position in Vietnam grew increasingly untenable as the war dragged on, and domestic opposition to the conflict mounted both in France and abroad. The French defeat at Dien Bien Phu in 1954, followed by the signing of the Geneva Accords, marked the end of French colonial rule in Vietnam and the beginning of a new phase of American involvement in the region.

The Geneva Accords and the division of Vietnam

The Geneva Accords of 1954 were a series of agreements negotiated between France, Vietnam, Laos, Cambodia, the Soviet Union, China, and the United States to resolve the conflict in Indochina and pave the way for a peaceful settlement of the region's political future. The accords, signed on July 21, 1954, in Geneva, Switzerland, laid out a framework for the temporary division of Vietnam along the 17th parallel, pending nationwide elections to reunify the country under a single government.

The Geneva Accords consisted of several key provisions, including the following:

1. Ceasefire: The signatories agreed to an immediate ceasefire and the withdrawal of all foreign military forces from Vietnam, Laos, and Cambodia. French colonial troops were to withdraw from northern Vietnam, while Viet Minh forces were to withdraw to the north of the 17th parallel.

2. Temporary division of Vietnam: Vietnam was to be temporarily divided along the 17th parallel, with the communist-led Democratic Republic of Vietnam (DRV) controlling the north and the US-backed State of Vietnam (SVN) controlling the south. The division was intended to be temporary, pending nationwide elections to be held within two years to reunify the country under a single government.

3. Neutralization of Laos and Cambodia: Laos and Cambodia were to be granted independence and neutrality, with their territorial integrity respected by all parties. The accords called for the withdrawal of all foreign troops from Laos and Cambodia and the establishment of neutral governments in both countries.

4. International supervision: The accords provided for the deployment of international supervisory commissions to oversee the implementation of the ceasefire and the withdrawal of foreign troops. The International Control Commission (ICC), composed of representatives from India, Canada, and Poland, was tasked with monitoring compliance with the accords and resolving disputes between the parties.

The Geneva Accords represented a diplomatic compromise aimed at ending the protracted conflict in Indochina and laying the groundwork for a peaceful resolution of the region's political future. However, the accords were also a reflection of the Cold War realities and the competing interests of the major powers involved, particularly the United States and the Soviet Union.

For the United States, the division of Vietnam was seen as a temporary expedient to prevent the spread of communism in Southeast Asia and maintain a foothold in the region pending the outcome of the nationwide elections. However, American policymakers were wary of the prospect of a communist takeover of South Vietnam and sought to bolster the government of Ngo Dinh Diem through military and economic assistance.

In the North, Ho Chi Minh and the communist leadership viewed the Geneva Accords as a stepping stone toward reunification and independence for Vietnam. Despite agreeing to the temporary division of the country, the DRV continued to pursue its goal of liberating the South and establishing a unified socialist Vietnam.

The failure to hold nationwide elections as stipulated in the Geneva Accords, due to opposition from the United States and South Vietnamese government, further deepened the divide between North and South Vietnam and set the stage for further conflict and confrontation. The temporary division of Vietnam would ultimately become permanent, leading to the escalation of the Vietnam War and the tragic loss of lives on all sides.

Chapter 4: Escalation

The Vietnam War was a conflict of escalating proportions, and Chapter 4 delves into two pivotal moments that dramatically increased the United States' involvement in the conflict: the early deployment of US advisors and the Gulf of Tonkin Incident, which led to the passage of the Gulf of Tonkin Resolution.

The Early Involvement of US Advisors

The early involvement of US advisors in Vietnam marked the beginning of America's entanglement in the conflict. Initially, US assistance to Vietnam was primarily advisory in nature, with the goal of supporting the South Vietnamese government's efforts to combat communist insurgents and maintain stability in the region.

1. Context and Background:

- By the late 1950s and early 1960s, South Vietnam, led by President Ngo Dinh Diem, faced significant challenges. Diem's government struggled to maintain control over the country amidst growing opposition and internal strife.

- The communist Viet Cong insurgency, supported by North Vietnam, posed a serious threat to the stability of South Vietnam. Diem's authoritarian rule and discriminatory policies exacerbated social tensions and fueled support for the Viet Cong among the rural population.

- In response to the deteriorating situation, the Eisenhower administration authorized the deployment of US military advisors to assist the South Vietnamese government in its counterinsurgency efforts. The advisors provided training, advice, and logistical support to the South Vietnamese armed forces.

2. Role of US Advisors:

- US military advisors, drawn from the Army Special Forces, the Central Intelligence Agency (CIA), and other branches of the military, played a crucial role in training and advising South Vietnamese troops.

- The advisors provided expertise in a wide range of areas, including counterinsurgency tactics, intelligence gathering, and civic action programs aimed at winning the hearts and minds of the Vietnamese population.

- Initially, the number of US advisors in Vietnam was relatively small, but their presence would gradually increase in the years to come as the conflict escalated.

3. Challenges and Limitations:

- The early involvement of US advisors faced numerous challenges and limitations. Cultural and language barriers often hindered communication and coordination between American advisors and their South Vietnamese counterparts.

- The political situation in South Vietnam was complex and volatile, with widespread corruption, incompetence, and factionalism within the South Vietnamese government undermining efforts to combat the communist insurgency.

- Despite the presence of US advisors, the South Vietnamese military struggled to effectively confront the Viet Cong, who continued to gain support and territory in rural areas.

4. Escalation of US Involvement:

- While the early deployment of US advisors was intended to support the South Vietnamese government and prevent the spread of communism, it would ultimately pave the way for deeper US involvement in the conflict.

- The advisors' role would evolve over time, from providing training and advice to actively participating in combat operations alongside South Vietnamese troops. This escalation of US involvement would culminate in the deployment of hundreds of thousands of American troops to Vietnam in the years that followed.

The Gulf of Tonkin Incident and the Passage of the Gulf of Tonkin Resolution

The Gulf of Tonkin Incident and the subsequent passage of the Gulf of Tonkin Resolution marked a significant escalation of US military involvement in Vietnam. These events, shrouded in controversy and misinformation, provided the justification for expanded US military action in Vietnam and laid the groundwork for the deepening of America's commitment to the conflict.

1. Background and Context:

- The Gulf of Tonkin Incident occurred in August 1964, amidst escalating tensions between the United States and North Vietnam. The incident took place in the waters of the Gulf of Tonkin, off the coast of North Vietnam, and involved alleged attacks on US Navy vessels by North Vietnamese patrol boats.

- The Johnson administration viewed the incident as an act of aggression by North Vietnam and an opportunity to justify a more aggressive US response to the communist threat in Southeast Asia.

2. Details of the Incident:

- On August 2, 1964, the USS Maddox, a US Navy destroyer, was conducting a routine patrol in international waters off the coast of North Vietnam when it allegedly came under attack by North Vietnamese torpedo boats. The incident resulted in no casualties or damage to the USS Maddox.

- Three days later, on August 4, 1964, another alleged incident occurred in the same area, involving the USS Maddox and the USS Turner Joy, another US Navy destroyer. Both ships reported being attacked by North Vietnamese patrol boats, although subsequent investigations raised doubts about the veracity of the second attack.

3. Response and Justification:

- In response to the Gulf of Tonkin Incident, President Lyndon B. Johnson sought congressional authorization to take whatever measures he deemed necessary to respond to the perceived threat posed by North

Vietnam. On August 7, 1964, Congress overwhelmingly passed the Gulf of Tonkin Resolution, granting the president broad powers to use military force in Vietnam without a formal declaration of war.

- The passage of the Gulf of Tonkin Resolution marked a significant escalation of US military involvement in Vietnam and signaled a shift toward a more aggressive and interventionist approach to the conflict.

4. Consequences and Impact:

- The Gulf of Tonkin Resolution had far-reaching consequences for the Vietnam War and for American society more broadly. It provided the legal and political justification for the escalation of US military action in Vietnam, including the deployment of hundreds of thousands of American troops and the intensification of bombing campaigns.

- The resolution also raised questions about the balance of power between the executive and legislative branches of government and the limits of presidential authority in times of war. It marked a departure from traditional constitutional norms and raised concerns about the erosion of congressional oversight and accountability.

In conclusion, Chapter 4 explores the early involvement of US advisors in Vietnam and the Gulf of Tonkin Incident, both of which were pivotal moments in the escalation of America's involvement in the conflict. These events laid the groundwork for deeper US military involvement in Vietnam and set the stage for the protracted and costly war that would follow.

Chapter 5: Military Strategies

The Vietnam War saw the implementation of various military strategies by both the United States and North Vietnam. Chapter 5 examines the contrasting approaches employed by the two sides, focusing on American tactics such as search and destroy missions, bombing campaigns, and the controversial use of defoliants like Agent Orange, as well as North Vietnamese strategies and guerrilla warfare tactics.

Examination of American Military Tactics

1. Search and Destroy:

- Search and destroy missions were a central component of the American military strategy in Vietnam. These operations involved sending US troops into suspected enemy-controlled areas to search for and engage Viet Cong or North Vietnamese forces.

- The objective of search and destroy missions was to locate and destroy enemy troops, supplies, and infrastructure, thereby weakening the communist insurgency and reducing their ability to operate in contested areas.

- However, search and destroy missions often proved to be ineffective and costly, as they frequently led to engagements with well-entrenched enemy forces and heavy casualties among American troops. Additionally, the practice of destroying villages suspected of harboring Viet Cong sympathizers alienated the civilian population and fueled resentment against US forces.

2. Bombing Campaigns:

- Bombing campaigns were a major component of American military strategy in Vietnam, aimed at destroying enemy infrastructure, disrupting supply lines, and demoralizing the North Vietnamese population.

- The United States conducted extensive bombing campaigns against North Vietnam, targeting strategic sites such as military installations, bridges, roads, and industrial facilities. The most infamous of these campaigns was Operation Rolling Thunder, which began in 1965 and lasted for three years.

- Despite the massive aerial bombardment, North Vietnam proved resilient, as it had dispersed its infrastructure and adopted decentralized methods of organization. The bombing campaigns caused widespread destruction and civilian casualties but failed to achieve their intended objectives of forcing North Vietnam to capitulate.

3. Use of Agent Orange:

- Agent Orange was a herbicide and defoliant used by the United States military to clear dense vegetation and deny cover to enemy forces. The herbicide contained toxic chemicals, including dioxin, which had devastating health and environmental effects.

- The widespread use of Agent Orange during the Vietnam War resulted in extensive environmental damage, destruction of agricultural land, and long-term health problems for both Vietnamese civilians and American veterans exposed to the chemical.

- Despite its intended purpose, Agent Orange failed to achieve its military objectives and instead caused significant harm to the Vietnamese people and the environment. Its use remains a controversial and contentious aspect of the Vietnam War, with lasting repercussions for all those affected.

Insights into North Vietnamese Strategies and Guerrilla Warfare Tactics

1. Guerrilla Warfare:

- The North Vietnamese forces, including the Viet Cong and the North Vietnamese Army (NVA), employed guerrilla warfare tactics against the better-equipped and more technologically advanced American military.

- Guerrilla warfare tactics relied on surprise attacks, hit-and-run ambushes, and the use of underground tunnels and hidden bunkers to evade detection and inflict maximum damage on enemy forces.

- The Viet Cong, in particular, were highly effective at blending in with the civilian population and exploiting the dense jungle terrain to launch attacks on US and South Vietnamese troops.

2. Protracted War Strategy:

- The North Vietnamese leadership, under Ho Chi Minh and General Vo Nguyen Giap, pursued a strategy of protracted war, aiming to outlast the superior firepower and resources of the United States and its allies.

- The protracted war strategy focused on wearing down the enemy through a combination of guerrilla tactics, political mobilization, and strategic patience. The North Vietnamese leadership understood that time was on their side and that they could win the war through attrition and perseverance.

- By maintaining popular support among the Vietnamese population and leveraging their ideological commitment to national liberation, the North Vietnamese were able to sustain their resistance against American military intervention.

3. Defensive Warfare:

- In addition to guerrilla tactics, the North Vietnamese forces also engaged in defensive warfare, fortifying key positions and launching counteroffensives to repel American advances.

- The Tet Offensive of 1968, launched by the Viet Cong and NVA forces, was a prime example of the North Vietnamese strategy of defensive warfare. Although the offensive ultimately failed to achieve its military objectives, it dealt a significant psychological blow to the United States and undermined public support for the war.

In conclusion, Chapter 5 provides a comprehensive analysis of the military strategies employed by both the United States and North Vietnam during the Vietnam War. While the United States relied on conventional tactics such as search and destroy missions, bombing campaigns, and the use of chemical defoliants, North Vietnam employed guerrilla warfare tactics, protracted war strategy, and defensive warfare to resist American military intervention. The chapter highlights the complex and asymmetrical nature of the conflict, as well as the enduring legacy of the Vietnam War on both sides.

Chapter 6: Home Front Divisions

The Vietnam War was not only fought on the battlefields of Southeast Asia but also on the home front in the United States. Chapter 6 explores the deep divisions within American society during the war years, focusing on the growing anti-war movement, its cultural impact, the proliferation of protests, and the influential role of media coverage in shaping public opinion.

The Growing Anti-War Movement in the United States

1. Origins and Evolution:

- The anti-war movement in the United States emerged in the early 1960s as opposition to the Vietnam War began to coalesce among various segments of society, including students, intellectuals, religious leaders, and civil rights activists.

- The movement was fueled by a combination of factors, including moral objections to the war, concerns about the draft and conscription policies, skepticism about the government's justifications for military intervention, and growing disillusionment with the conduct of the war.

- As the war dragged on and casualties mounted, opposition to the conflict grew increasingly vocal and widespread, attracting support from a diverse array of individuals and organizations across the political spectrum.

2. Key Players and Organizations:

- The anti-war movement encompassed a broad spectrum of individuals and organizations, ranging from student activists and grassroots peace groups to established civil rights organizations and religious denominations.

- Prominent figures in the anti-war movement included leaders such as Dr. Martin Luther King Jr., Senator George McGovern, and activist groups like Students for a Democratic Society (SDS), the Vietnam Veterans Against the War (VVAW), and the Women Strike for Peace (WSP).

- These organizations organized protests, rallies, teach-ins, and acts of civil disobedience to mobilize public opposition to the war and pressure the government to change its policies.

3. Tactics and Strategies:

- The anti-war movement employed a variety of tactics and strategies to raise awareness about the war and mobilize public opposition. These included mass demonstrations, draft resistance, conscientious objection, draft card burning, sit-ins, and boycotts of companies perceived to be profiting from the war.

- The movement also utilized alternative forms of media and communication, such as underground newspapers, pamphlets, posters, and music, to disseminate its message and challenge official narratives about the war.

Cultural Impact, Protests, and the Role of Media Coverage

1. Cultural Impact:

- The Vietnam War had a profound impact on American culture, shaping the music, art, literature, and film of the era. Artists, musicians, and writers responded to the war with a wave of protest and dissent, producing works that reflected the growing anti-war sentiment in society.

- Protest songs such as Bob Dylan's "Blowin' in the Wind," Creedence Clearwater Revival's "Fortunate Son," and Edwin Starr's "War" became anthems of the anti-war movement, expressing the anger, frustration, and disillusionment felt by many Americans.

- Films like "Apocalypse Now," "Platoon," and "Full Metal Jacket" depicted the brutality and futility of the war, challenging conventional notions of heroism and patriotism.

2. Protests and Demonstrations:

- The Vietnam War sparked a wave of protests and demonstrations across the United States, as millions of Americans took to the streets to voice their opposition to the conflict.

- The largest and most famous of these protests was the Moratorium to End the War in Vietnam, held on October 15, 1969. Organized by a coalition of anti-war groups, the moratorium brought together millions of protesters in cities and towns across the country to demand an immediate end to the war.

- Other notable protests included the March on the Pentagon in 1967, the Kent State shootings in 1970, and the May Day protests in 1971, which saw thousands of demonstrators occupy the streets of Washington, D.C., in a mass act of civil disobedience.

3. Role of Media Coverage:

- The Vietnam War was the first conflict to be extensively covered by the media, thanks to advances in technology such as television and satellite communication.

- Media coverage of the war played a pivotal role in shaping public opinion and influencing government policy. Images of combat footage, casualty reports, and interviews with soldiers and civilians brought the reality of the war into the living rooms of millions of Americans, sparking outrage and prompting calls for an end to the conflict.

- Journalists such as Walter Cronkite, David Halberstam, and Neil Sheehan played a crucial role in exposing the truth about the war and challenging official narratives promoted by the government.

In conclusion, Chapter 6 explores the divisions within American society during the Vietnam War, focusing on the growing anti-war movement and its cultural impact, protests, and the influential role of media coverage in shaping public opinion. The chapter highlights the profound social and political upheaval caused by the war and its lasting impact on American society and politics.

Chapter 7: Tet Offensive

The Tet Offensive of 1968 was a turning point in the Vietnam War, with far-reaching implications for both military strategy and public opinion. Chapter 7 delves into the significance of the Tet Offensive, analyzing its impact on shifting public opinion, military strategy, and political decision-making in the United States.

The Significance of the Tet Offensive in Shifting Public Opinion

1. Background and Context:

    - The Tet Offensive was a coordinated series of surprise attacks launched by the Viet Cong and North Vietnamese forces against South Vietnamese cities, towns, and military installations during the Lunar New Year holiday of Tet in January 1968.

    - The offensive took US and South Vietnamese forces by surprise, as it violated a traditional ceasefire observed during the holiday season. The scale and intensity of the attacks shocked both military commanders and the American public, who had been led to believe that the enemy was on the verge of defeat.

    2. Psychological Impact:

    - The Tet Offensive shattered the perception of progress and imminent victory propagated by the Johnson administration and military officials. Images of intense urban combat, casualties, and destruction broadcast on television screens across America undermined confidence in the government's assurances of success.

    - The offensive exposed the wide gap between official pronouncements and the grim reality of the war on the ground, leading many Americans to question the credibility of their leaders and the justification for continued military involvement in Vietnam.

    3. Media Coverage:

- Media coverage of the Tet Offensive played a crucial role in shaping public perceptions of the war. Journalists such as Walter Cronkite, reporting from the front lines in Vietnam, provided unfiltered accounts of the fighting and its human cost, challenging official narratives of progress and success.

- The stark contrast between the upbeat assessments of military officials and the grim reality depicted in news reports fueled skepticism and distrust among the American public, eroding support for the war effort and intensifying calls for a change in policy.

Analysis of Its Impact on Military Strategy and Political Decision-Making

1. Reassessment of Military Strategy:

- The Tet Offensive forced US military commanders to reassess their assumptions and strategies in Vietnam. The coordinated nature and scope of the attacks exposed vulnerabilities in American military planning and intelligence-gathering capabilities, prompting a reevaluation of counterinsurgency tactics and force deployment.

- The offensive demonstrated the resilience and determination of the Viet Cong and North Vietnamese forces, challenging the prevailing notion that the enemy was on the brink of defeat. US military leaders recognized the need for a more flexible and nuanced approach to counterinsurgency warfare, focusing on winning the hearts and minds of the Vietnamese population rather than simply targeting enemy fighters.

2. Political Fallout:

- The Tet Offensive had profound political implications in the United States, exacerbating divisions within the Johnson administration and fueling opposition to the war among policymakers, legislators, and the general public.

- President Lyndon B. Johnson's handling of the Tet Offensive came under intense scrutiny, as his administration struggled to provide a coherent and reassuring response to the crisis. The perceived failure of leadership and mismanagement of the war eroded Johnson's credibility and undermined public confidence in his administration.

- The Tet Offensive also galvanized anti-war sentiment within the Democratic Party, leading to growing calls for a reassessment of US policy in Vietnam and the eventual withdrawal of American troops.

3. Impact on Political Decision-Making:

- The Tet Offensive accelerated the unraveling of the Johnson administration's Vietnam policy and contributed to Johnson's decision not to seek reelection in 1968. The mounting pressure from within his own party, combined with the growing anti-war movement and public disillusionment, forced Johnson to announce a partial bombing halt and open negotiations with North Vietnam.

- The offensive also influenced the outcome of the 1968 presidential election, with the Republican candidate, Richard Nixon, capitalizing on public dissatisfaction with Johnson's handling of the war and promising to bring an end to the conflict through a policy of "peace with honor."

In conclusion, Chapter 7 examines the significance of the Tet Offensive in shifting public opinion, reshaping military strategy, and influencing political decision-making in the United States. The offensive exposed the gap between official rhetoric and the harsh realities of the war, fueling disillusionment and dissent among the American public and hastening the end of US involvement in Vietnam.

Chapter 8: Nixon's War

President Richard Nixon's approach to the Vietnam War marked a significant shift in American strategy, characterized by the implementation of Vietnamization and the escalation of covert bombing campaigns in neighboring countries. Chapter 8 explores Nixon's Vietnamization policy, the withdrawal of US troops, and the secret bombing campaigns in Cambodia and Laos.

Nixon's Vietnamization Policy and the Withdrawal of US Troops

1. Introduction of Vietnamization:

- Nixon took office in January 1969, inheriting a deeply divided nation and an increasingly unpopular war in Vietnam. Seeking to extricate the United States from the conflict while still maintaining a semblance of credibility and honor, Nixon introduced the policy of Vietnamization.

- Vietnamization aimed to shift the burden of combat operations from American to South Vietnamese forces, gradually reducing US troop levels and transferring responsibility for the defense of South Vietnam to the South Vietnamese government and military.

2. Key Components of Vietnamization:

- Under Vietnamization, US troops were gradually withdrawn from Vietnam, with the goal of reducing American forces by transferring combat responsibilities to South Vietnamese troops.

- At the same time, Nixon sought to strengthen the South Vietnamese military's capabilities through increased training, equipment, and logistical support. The United States also provided financial aid and technical assistance to improve the South Vietnamese government's capacity to govern and provide essential services to its population.

3. Challenges and Limitations:

- Despite the implementation of Vietnamization, the policy faced numerous challenges and limitations. The South Vietnamese military, plagued by corruption, inefficiency, and low morale, struggled to fill the void left by departing American troops.

- The withdrawal of US forces also created security vacuums in certain areas, allowing the Viet Cong and North Vietnamese forces to exploit weaknesses and launch attacks with impunity.

- Additionally, the policy of Vietnamization did little to address the underlying political, economic, and social grievances that fueled the communist insurgency, leading to continued instability and unrest in South Vietnam.

The Secret Bombing Campaigns in Cambodia and Laos

1. Expansion of the War:

- In addition to implementing Vietnamization, Nixon pursued a policy of expanding the war into neighboring countries, particularly Cambodia and Laos, in an effort to disrupt North Vietnamese supply lines and sanctuary areas.

- Beginning in 1969, the Nixon administration authorized a series of secret bombing campaigns, codenamed Operation Menu in Cambodia and Operation Steel Tiger in Laos, targeting suspected Viet Cong and North Vietnamese bases along the Ho Chi Minh Trail.

2. Strategic Rationale:

- The secret bombing campaigns in Cambodia and Laos were driven by the Nixon administration's belief that cutting off the flow of men and supplies along the Ho Chi Minh Trail would weaken the communist insurgency and hasten the end of the war.

- By expanding the scope of military operations beyond the borders of Vietnam, Nixon sought to apply pressure on North Vietnam and force the communist leadership to come to the negotiating table on US terms.

3. Humanitarian and Environmental Consequences:

- The secret bombing campaigns in Cambodia and Laos had devastating humanitarian and environmental consequences. The intense bombing raids resulted in widespread destruction of villages, displacement of civilians, and loss of life.

- The use of highly explosive ordnance, including cluster bombs and napalm, caused extensive damage to the environment, forests, and agricultural land, poisoning water sources and disrupting local ecosystems.

4. Political Fallout:

- The secret bombing campaigns in Cambodia and Laos sparked outrage and condemnation both domestically and internationally. The Nixon administration's covert actions violated the sovereignty of these neutral countries and drew criticism from Congress, the media, and the international community.

- The revelation of the secret bombing campaigns further eroded public trust in the government's conduct of the war and fueled anti-war sentiment, contributing to growing calls for an end to US military intervention in Southeast Asia.

In conclusion, Chapter 8 examines Nixon's approach to the Vietnam War, focusing on the implementation of Vietnamization and the escalation of secret bombing campaigns in Cambodia and Laos. While Vietnamization aimed to reduce US involvement in the conflict, the expansion of military operations into neighboring countries raised ethical, legal, and strategic concerns, exacerbating the human and environmental toll of the war and fueling opposition to Nixon's policies both at home and abroad.

Chapter 9: The Peace Process

The Vietnam War was a protracted and bloody conflict that left deep scars on both the Vietnamese and American societies. Chapter 9 explores the efforts to end the war through negotiations in Paris, led by National Security Advisor Henry Kissinger. It also examines the challenges and setbacks encountered in reaching a peace agreement that would bring an end to the fighting.

Negotiations in Paris and the Role of Henry Kissinger

1. Background and Context:

- By the late 1960s, the United States was embroiled in a costly and increasingly unpopular war in Vietnam. With mounting casualties and growing public discontent, there was a growing recognition within the Johnson and Nixon administrations of the need to find a diplomatic solution to the conflict.

- In 1968, secret talks between US and North Vietnamese officials began in Paris, mediated by French diplomat Jules Moch. These initial discussions laid the groundwork for more formal negotiations aimed at reaching a peace agreement.

2. Appointment of Henry Kissinger:

- In 1969, President Richard Nixon appointed Henry Kissinger as his National Security Advisor, tasking him with overseeing the administration's efforts to end the war in Vietnam. Kissinger, a skilled diplomat and strategist, played a central role in shaping US policy and negotiating with North Vietnamese representatives.

- Kissinger's approach to diplomacy was characterized by a combination of pragmatism, flexibility, and realpolitik, as he sought to balance US strategic interests with the need for a peaceful resolution to the conflict.

3. Paris Peace Talks:

- The formal peace negotiations in Paris began in 1969, with representatives from the United States, North Vietnam, South Vietnam, and the National Liberation Front (NLF) of South Vietnam participating in the talks. The negotiations were conducted under the auspices of the International Control Commission (ICC) and chaired by US Ambassador William J. Porter.

- Kissinger engaged in a series of secret meetings with North Vietnamese negotiators, including Le Duc Tho, to explore possible avenues for a peace agreement. Despite initial progress, the negotiations would be marked by protracted delays, deadlock, and mutual mistrust.

Challenges and Setbacks in Reaching a Peace Agreement

1. Military Escalation and Stalemate:

- Despite the ongoing negotiations in Paris, the war in Vietnam continued unabated, with both sides escalating their military operations in a bid to gain leverage at the negotiating table.

- The North Vietnamese launched a series of offensives, including the Easter Offensive in 1972, aimed at breaking the deadlock and forcing the United States to make concessions. Meanwhile, the Nixon administration responded with a massive bombing campaign against North Vietnam, including the infamous Christmas Bombing of Hanoi and Haiphong.

2. Deadlock and Stalemate:

The Paris Peace Talks were marked by prolonged periods of deadlock and stalemate, as both sides remained entrenched in their positions and unwilling to compromise on key issues such as the withdrawal of US troops, the political future of South Vietnam, and the status of POWs.

- Despite the efforts of Kissinger and other negotiators to bridge the gap between the two sides, fundamental disagreements over the terms of a peace settlement, as well as domestic political considerations, impeded progress and prolonged the conflict.

3. Watergate Scandal and Political Turmoil:

- The Watergate scandal, which engulfed the Nixon administration in 1972-1974, further complicated efforts to end the war in Vietnam. The scandal, which involved illegal activities and abuses of power by members of the Nixon administration, undermined Nixon's credibility and distracted attention from the peace negotiations.

- The political turmoil surrounding Watergate weakened Nixon's ability to pursue a coherent and consistent foreign policy, as his administration became increasingly consumed by the unfolding scandal and the threat of impeachment.

4. Final Agreement and Withdrawal:

- Despite the challenges and setbacks, the Paris Peace Talks eventually resulted in the signing of the Paris Peace Accords on January 27, 1973. The agreement called for a ceasefire, the withdrawal of US troops from Vietnam, the release of prisoners of war, and the establishment of a political process to resolve the conflict in South Vietnam.

- In accordance with the terms of the agreement, US forces began withdrawing from Vietnam, marking the beginning of the end of America's direct involvement in the war. However, the peace was short-lived, as the conflict in Vietnam would continue for another two years before the fall of Saigon in 1975.

In conclusion, Chapter 9 examines the efforts to end the Vietnam War through negotiations in Paris, led by Henry Kissinger, and the challenges and setbacks encountered in reaching a peace agreement. Despite the eventual signing of the Paris Peace Accords, the war would continue for several more years, underscoring the complexities and difficulties of resolving the conflict through diplomacy.

Chapter 10: Fall of Saigon

The fall of Saigon on April 30, 1975, marked the end of the Vietnam War and the culmination of decades of conflict and turmoil in Vietnam. Chapter 10 explores the final days of the war, the evacuation of American personnel, and the repercussions of the fall of Saigon for Vietnam and the region.

The Final Days of the War and the Evacuation of American Personnel

1. Collapse of South Vietnam:

- By early 1975, the situation in South Vietnam had become increasingly dire. The South Vietnamese military, plagued by corruption, incompetence, and low morale, was unable to withstand the relentless onslaught of North Vietnamese forces.

- In March 1975, the North Vietnamese launched a massive offensive, rapidly advancing southward and capturing key cities and strategic positions. Despite desperate attempts by South Vietnamese forces and US advisors to stem the tide, the collapse of the South Vietnamese government became inevitable.

2. Evacuation Preparations:

- As the situation in South Vietnam deteriorated rapidly, the United States began making preparations for the evacuation of American personnel and at-risk Vietnamese allies. Operation Frequent Wind, the largest helicopter evacuation in history, was launched to evacuate US citizens, embassy staff, and Vietnamese refugees from Saigon.

3. Chaos and Panic:

- The evacuation of Saigon descended into chaos and panic as thousands of people sought to flee the city before the advancing North Vietnamese forces. Helicopters shuttled back and forth between the US embassy compound and the ships waiting offshore, frantically airlifting evacuees to safety.

- Scenes of desperation and confusion unfolded as crowds of people clamored to board the helicopters, with many Vietnamese nationals clinging to the skids or hanging onto the landing gear in a desperate bid to escape.

4. Fall of the US Embassy:

- On April 30, 1975, North Vietnamese forces breached the perimeter of the US embassy compound in Saigon, signaling the final collapse of the South Vietnamese government. In a dramatic and chaotic scene, the remaining American personnel and Vietnamese refugees were evacuated by helicopter from the embassy rooftop.

5. End of the War:

- With the fall of Saigon, the Vietnam War came to a sudden and ignominious end. North Vietnamese troops entered the city, marking the reunification of Vietnam under communist rule and the culmination of decades of struggle for independence and reunification.

Repercussions of the Fall of Saigon for Vietnam and the Region

1. Humanitarian Crisis:

- The fall of Saigon triggered a humanitarian crisis as thousands of Vietnamese nationals, fearing reprisals from the new communist regime, sought to escape the country by any means possible. Many risked their lives in overcrowded boats and makeshift rafts, braving treacherous seas in search of refuge in neighboring countries.

2. Political Fallout:

- The fall of Saigon had far-reaching political repercussions for Vietnam and the region. In the immediate aftermath of the war, the communist government of North Vietnam moved quickly to consolidate its control over the entire country, implementing a program of socialist transformation and national reconciliation.

- The defeat of South Vietnam also had geopolitical implications, leading to a realignment of power dynamics in Southeast Asia and emboldening communist movements in neighboring countries such as Laos and Cambodia.

3. Legacy of the Vietnam War:

- The fall of Saigon marked the end of one of the most divisive and contentious conflicts in modern history. The Vietnam War had claimed the lives of millions of Vietnamese civilians and soldiers, as well as tens of thousands of American troops.

- The war left deep scars on Vietnamese society and the American psyche, shaping political attitudes and cultural perceptions for generations to come. It also sparked soul-searching and reflection in the United States, leading to a reevaluation of US foreign policy and military interventionism.

4. Reconciliation and Reconstruction:

- In the years following the fall of Saigon, Vietnam embarked on a process of national reconstruction and reconciliation. The government pursued economic reforms and opened up to foreign investment, seeking to rebuild the war-torn country and improve the standard of living for its people.

- Despite the challenges of post-war reconstruction, Vietnam has experienced remarkable economic growth and development in the decades since the war, emerging as one of the fastest-growing economies in Southeast Asia.

In conclusion, Chapter 10 examines the final days of the Vietnam War and the fall of Saigon, highlighting the chaos and desperation of the evacuation efforts and the far-reaching repercussions of the war for Vietnam and the region. The fall of Saigon marked the end of a tragic chapter in Vietnamese history but also paved the way for a new era of reconciliation, reconstruction, and national renewal.

Chapter 11: Legacy of the War

The Vietnam War left a profound and enduring legacy that continues to shape the cultural, political, and psychological landscapes of Vietnam, the United States, and other countries involved in the conflict. Chapter 11 delves into the long-term impacts of the war and reflects on its cultural, political, and psychological legacies.

Examination of the Long-Term Impacts

1. Vietnam:

- The Vietnam War had devastating consequences for Vietnam, both during the conflict and in its aftermath. The war resulted in millions of deaths, widespread destruction of infrastructure, and long-lasting environmental damage from the extensive use of herbicides like Agent Orange.

- Despite these challenges, Vietnam embarked on a path of national reconstruction and economic development in the years following the war. The government implemented economic reforms and opened up to foreign investment, leading to rapid industrialization and urbanization.

- However, the war's legacy continues to cast a shadow over Vietnamese society, with many communities still grappling with the physical and psychological scars of the conflict. The ongoing health effects of Agent Orange exposure and unexploded ordnance pose significant challenges to public health and safety in affected areas.

2. United States:

- The Vietnam War had a profound impact on American society, politics, and culture. The war shattered the myth of American invincibility and undermined public confidence in the government's ability to pursue military intervention abroad.

- The war also exacerbated social divisions within the United States, fueling protests, civil unrest, and political polarization. The anti-war movement, fueled by opposition to the draft and concerns about the morality and efficacy of US foreign policy, mobilized millions of Americans in support of peace and withdrawal from Vietnam.

- The Vietnam War prompted a period of soul-searching and reflection in the United States, leading to a reassessment of America's role in the world and a shift towards a more cautious and pragmatic approach to foreign policy.

3. Other Countries Involved:

- The Vietnam War had ripple effects that extended beyond Vietnam and the United States, impacting other countries involved in the conflict, such as Cambodia and Laos. The secret bombing campaigns in these countries, aimed at disrupting North Vietnamese supply lines, resulted in widespread destruction and loss of life.

- In Cambodia, the bombing raids destabilized the country and contributed to the rise of the Khmer Rouge regime, which would go on to perpetrate genocide and mass atrocities against its own people.

- In Laos, the unexploded ordnance left behind by the bombing campaigns continues to pose a significant threat to civilian populations, hindering economic development and causing countless casualties each year.

Reflections on the War's Cultural, Political, and Psychological Legacies

1. Cultural Legacy:

- The Vietnam War left an indelible mark on popular culture, inspiring a rich and diverse body of literature, film, music, and art that continues to resonate with audiences around the world. Works such as Tim O'Brien's "The Things They Carried," Francis Ford Coppola's "Apocalypse Now," and Bob Dylan's "Masters of War" capture the brutality and absurdity of war and its impact on individuals and societies.

- The war also gave rise to a generation of artists, writers, and filmmakers who sought to grapple with the moral and existential questions raised by the conflict, exploring themes of trauma, memory, and reconciliation in their work.

2. Political Legacy:

- The Vietnam War transformed the political landscape of the United States, leading to a profound loss of trust in government institutions and a growing skepticism of military interventionism. The war's legacy continues to influence debates over US foreign policy, defense spending, and military intervention abroad.

- The lessons of Vietnam have shaped subsequent American military interventions, with policymakers and military leaders mindful of the need to avoid another quagmire and the risks of "mission creep" in conflicts such as Afghanistan and Iraq.

3. Psychological Legacy:

- The Vietnam War left deep psychological scars on those who lived through it, both in Vietnam and the United States. Veterans of the war experienced high rates of post-traumatic stress disorder (PTSD), depression, and substance abuse, with many struggling to reintegrate into civilian life after returning home.

- In Vietnam, the war's legacy continues to haunt survivors and their families, with memories of loss, displacement, and trauma passed down through generations. Efforts to address the psychological wounds of war, including counseling, support groups, and memorialization, remain ongoing in both countries.

In conclusion, Chapter 11 reflects on the enduring legacy of the Vietnam War, examining its long-term impacts on Vietnam, the United States, and other countries involved in the conflict. From the physical and psychological scars left behind in Vietnam to the cultural and political reverberations felt in the United States and beyond, the Vietnam War continues to shape our understanding of war, memory, and the human experience.

Chapter 12: Veterans' Stories

The Vietnam War left an indelible mark on the lives of those who fought in it, both American veterans and Vietnamese survivors. Chapter 12 delves into the personal narratives of veterans from both sides of the conflict, offering insights into their experiences, struggles, and perspectives on the war.

American Veterans' Stories

1. Joe's Story:

- Joe enlisted in the US Army in 1967, eager to serve his country and defend against the spread of communism in Southeast Asia. Deployed to Vietnam as a young infantryman, Joe quickly found himself thrust into the brutal realities of war.

- Joe vividly recalls the intense heat, humidity, and pervasive sense of fear and uncertainty that permeated the jungles of Vietnam. He describes the chaos and confusion of combat, the camaraderie forged with his fellow soldiers, and the moments of sheer terror as he came under enemy fire.

- Like many veterans, Joe struggled to reconcile his experiences in Vietnam with the ideals of patriotism and duty instilled in him from a young age. He grappled with feelings of guilt, shame, and anger over the senseless violence and loss of life he witnessed and participated in during the war.

2. Mary's Story:

- Mary served as a nurse in Vietnam, caring for wounded soldiers at a field hospital near the front lines. Her experiences provided her with a unique perspective on the human cost of war and the toll it took on both soldiers and civilians.

- Mary recalls the harrowing sight of young men brought in with horrific injuries, their bodies mangled by shrapnel, bullets, and explosives. She describes the desperate efforts of medical personnel to save lives amid the chaos and carnage of the battlefield.

- Despite the overwhelming challenges and emotional toll of her work, Mary found solace in the bonds of friendship and solidarity forged with her fellow nurses and soldiers. She remains haunted by the memories of those she could not save and the faces of the wounded and dying who passed through her care.

Vietnamese Survivors' Stories

1. Thanh's Story:

- Thanh was just a child when the war engulfed his village in the countryside of South Vietnam. Forced to flee his home with his family to escape the violence and destruction, Thanh witnessed firsthand the horrors of war and displacement.

- Thanh recalls the terror of hiding in makeshift shelters as bombs rained down from above, the sound of gunfire echoing in the distance. He remembers the fear and uncertainty of not knowing whether he would ever see his home or loved ones again.

- Despite the trauma and loss he endured, Thanh found resilience and hope in the midst of adversity. He rebuilt his life from the ruins of war, finding purpose and meaning in his work and relationships with others.

2. Linh's Story:

- Linh's family lived in the heart of Saigon, where they ran a small business selling goods in the bustling market. As the war drew closer to the city, Linh and her family were forced to flee their home and seek refuge in overcrowded shelters.

- Linh vividly recalls the chaos and confusion of the final days of the war, as North Vietnamese troops closed in on the city and panic gripped the population. She remembers the long lines at evacuation points, the sound of gunfire in the streets, and the desperate scramble to find safety amid the chaos.

- Despite the trauma and upheaval of the war, Linh remains grateful for the opportunity to rebuild her life in the aftermath of the conflict. She cherishes the memories of her family and community, drawing strength from their resilience and determination to persevere in the face of adversity.

Insights into the Experiences of Soldiers on Both Sides of the Conflict

1. Shared Humanity:

- Despite their differences in background, culture, and ideology, American veterans and Vietnamese survivors share a common humanity forged by the crucible of war. Both groups experienced the trauma, fear, and loss that are inherent to armed conflict, as well as the resilience, courage, and camaraderie that sustain individuals in times of crisis.

- Through their stories, veterans and survivors offer powerful reminders of the human cost of war and the enduring bonds of compassion and solidarity that transcend national boundaries and political divides.

2. Lessons Learned:

- The personal narratives of veterans and survivors provide valuable insights into the complexities and contradictions of war, challenging simplistic narratives of heroism and villainy. They underscore the need for empathy, understanding, and reconciliation in the aftermath of conflict, as well as the importance of remembering and honoring the sacrifices of those who served and suffered.

- By bearing witness to their experiences and sharing their stories, veterans and survivors contribute to the ongoing process of healing, reconciliation, and peacebuilding in Vietnam and beyond. Their voices serve as a powerful testament to the resilience of the human spirit and the enduring quest for justice, dignity, and freedom in the face of adversity.

In conclusion, Chapter 12 offers a poignant exploration of the personal narratives of American veterans and Vietnamese survivors, providing insights into their experiences, struggles, and perspectives on the Vietnam War. Through their stories, veterans and survivors bear witness to the human cost of war and the enduring legacy of courage, resilience, and hope in the face of adversity. Their voices remind us of the importance of empathy, understanding, and reconciliation in the aftermath of conflict, and the imperative of honoring the sacrifices of those who served and suffered.

Chapter 13: Healing and Reconciliation

The wounds of war run deep, but so too does the human capacity for healing and reconciliation. Chapter 13 delves into the efforts to address the trauma of the Vietnam War and reconcile differences between former enemies, examining the role of memorialization and commemoration in this ongoing process.

Efforts to Address the Trauma of War

1. Veterans' Support Services:

- In the decades following the Vietnam War, a range of support services and resources have been established to assist veterans in coping with the physical, emotional, and psychological wounds of war. These services include counseling, therapy, support groups, and access to healthcare for conditions such as post-traumatic stress disorder (PTSD) and Agent Orange exposure.

- Organizations such as the Department of Veterans Affairs (VA) in the United States and veterans' associations in Vietnam provide assistance and advocacy for veterans and their families, helping to address the long-term effects of their military service and facilitate their reintegration into civilian life.

2. Reconciliation Initiatives:

- Despite the deep divisions and animosities that characterized the Vietnam War, efforts to promote reconciliation and healing have emerged in the post-war era. Veterans from both sides of the conflict have come together in forums and dialogues aimed at fostering understanding, empathy, and forgiveness.

- Programs such as the Vietnam Veterans of America Foundation's (VVAF) "War Legacies Project" and the Vietnam Friendship Village Project seek to promote reconciliation and friendship between

American veterans and Vietnamese survivors through humanitarian aid, cultural exchange, and grassroots initiatives.

3. Cross-Cultural Dialogue:

- Cross-cultural dialogue and exchange have played a crucial role in fostering reconciliation and understanding between former enemies. Through initiatives such as exchange programs, educational workshops, and joint commemorative events, veterans and survivors have had the opportunity to share their stories, experiences, and perspectives with one another.

- These dialogues provide a space for mutual recognition and acknowledgment of the pain, suffering, and loss experienced by all parties during the war, fostering empathy, compassion, and solidarity across national and cultural boundaries.

Examination of Memorialization and Commemoration Efforts

1. War Memorials:

- War memorials serve as physical reminders of the sacrifices made by those who served and died in the Vietnam War. From the Vietnam Veterans Memorial Wall in Washington, D.C., to the War Remnants Museum in Ho Chi Minh City, these monuments and museums provide spaces for reflection, remembrance, and tribute.

- The Vietnam Veterans Memorial Wall, designed by Maya Lin, stands as a solemn tribute to the more than 58,000 American servicemen and women who lost their lives in the war. Its stark black granite surface, inscribed with the names of the fallen, invites visitors to pause, reflect, and pay their respects.

2. Reconciliation Memorials:

- In addition to traditional war memorials, efforts have been made to establish reconciliation memorials that promote healing and understanding between former enemies. These memorials often commemorate the shared suffering and resilience of all those affected by the war, regardless of nationality or allegiance.

- The My Lai Peace Park in Vietnam, built on the site of the infamous My Lai massacre, serves as a poignant reminder of the tragedy of war and the importance of reconciliation and forgiveness. The park features memorials, exhibits, and educational programs that promote peace, reconciliation, and healing.

3. Commemorative Events:

- Commemorative events and ceremonies play a vital role in honoring the memory of those who served and died in the Vietnam War and promoting reconciliation and healing among survivors and their families. These events bring together veterans, survivors, policymakers, and community members to reflect on the legacy of the war and its impact on individuals and societies.

- Anniversaries such as Veterans Day in the United States and Reunification Day in Vietnam provide opportunities for communities to come together in remembrance and solidarity, reaffirming their commitment to peace, reconciliation, and mutual understanding.

4. Educational Initiatives:

- Educational initiatives aimed at raising awareness and understanding of the Vietnam War and its legacies have played a crucial role in promoting reconciliation and healing. These initiatives include curriculum development, educational resources, and outreach programs designed to engage students, educators, and the broader public in meaningful dialogue and reflection.

- The Vietnam Center and Archive at Texas Tech University and the Vietnam War Legacy Project at the University of Southern California are examples of institutions dedicated to preserving and disseminating the history and memory of the war through research, teaching, and public outreach.

In conclusion, Chapter 13 explores the efforts to address the trauma of the Vietnam War and promote healing and reconciliation between former enemies. From veterans' support services and reconciliation initiatives to memorialization and commemoration efforts, these initiatives seek to honor the memory of those who served and died in the war and foster understanding, empathy, and forgiveness among survivors and their families. By acknowledging the pain and suffering experienced by all parties and working together to build a more peaceful and just future, communities affected by the Vietnam War continue to demonstrate the enduring power of resilience, compassion, and reconciliation.

Chapter 14: Lessons Learned

The Vietnam War stands as a watershed moment in American history, reshaping the nation's understanding of war, foreign policy, and military strategy. Chapter 14 reflects on the lessons of the Vietnam War for US foreign policy and military strategy, as well as its impact on subsequent conflicts and interventions.

Reflections on the Vietnam War's Lessons

1. Limited War Doctrine:
   - The Vietnam War challenged prevailing notions of warfighting and military strategy, prompting a reevaluation of the concept of limited war. The conflict exposed the limitations of conventional military force in countering unconventional insurgencies and guerrilla warfare tactics employed by the Viet Cong and North Vietnamese forces.
   - The doctrine of limited war, which emphasized the use of measured force and the avoidance of escalation to achieve political objectives, came under scrutiny in the wake of the Vietnam War. Policymakers and military leaders questioned the feasibility and effectiveness of waging limited wars in the face of determined and resilient adversaries.

   2. Counterinsurgency Strategy:
   - The Vietnam War underscored the importance of developing effective counterinsurgency strategies to combat irregular warfare and insurgent movements. The failure of US forces to adequately address the underlying political, economic, and social grievances that fueled the communist insurgency in Vietnam highlighted the need for a comprehensive approach to counterinsurgency.
   - The lessons of Vietnam informed subsequent efforts to refine counterinsurgency doctrine and tactics, emphasizing the importance of winning the hearts and minds of the local population, building

indigenous security forces, and addressing root causes of instability and conflict.

3. Civil-Military Relations:

- The Vietnam War strained civil-military relations in the United States, exposing tensions and divisions between civilian policymakers and military leaders over strategy, objectives, and the conduct of the war. The erosion of trust and confidence between political and military leaders contributed to the breakdown of decision-making processes and hindered effective coordination and execution of military operations.

- The Vietnam War prompted a reexamination of the role of the military in policymaking and the need for greater civilian oversight and accountability in matters of national security. Efforts were made to strengthen civilian control of the military and improve mechanisms for interagency coordination and cooperation.

4. Public Opinion and War Powers:

- The Vietnam War catalyzed a shift in public opinion and attitudes towards military interventionism and executive war powers. The widespread protests, demonstrations, and civil unrest that swept across the United States during the war reflected growing disillusionment and opposition to US involvement in Vietnam.

- The Vietnam War prompted Congress to assert its constitutional authority over war powers, culminating in the passage of the War Powers Resolution in 1973. The resolution sought to limit the president's ability to commit US forces to combat without congressional authorization, reflecting concerns about the executive branch's unchecked authority to wage war.

Analysis of its Impact on Subsequent Conflicts and Interventions

1. Post-Vietnam Conflicts:

- The Vietnam War had a profound impact on subsequent US military interventions and conflicts, shaping attitudes and approaches towards foreign policy and military interventionism. The "Vietnam Syndrome," characterized by a reluctance to engage in large-scale military interventions abroad, influenced decision-making in conflicts such as the Gulf War, Iraq War, and Afghanistan War.

- Policymakers and military leaders sought to avoid the mistakes and pitfalls of Vietnam, adopting strategies and tactics aimed at minimizing casualties, limiting duration, and achieving clear and achievable objectives. However, the legacy of Vietnam continued to loom large, shaping debates and controversies surrounding the use of force and the costs of war.

2. Guerrilla Warfare and Asymmetric Conflict:

- The Vietnam War demonstrated the effectiveness of guerrilla warfare and asymmetric tactics in countering conventional military forces, influencing subsequent insurgencies and conflicts around the world. Lessons learned from Vietnam informed the strategies and tactics of insurgent groups and non-state actors seeking to challenge more powerful adversaries.

- The rise of non-state actors and transnational terrorist organizations in the post-Cold War era, such as al-Qaeda and ISIS, highlighted the enduring relevance of guerrilla warfare and irregular tactics in modern conflicts. The Vietnam War served as a case study for understanding the dynamics of asymmetric conflict and the challenges of counterinsurgency operations in complex and contested environments.

3. Humanitarian Intervention and Nation-Building:

- The Vietnam War raised important questions about the ethics and efficacy of humanitarian intervention and nation-building efforts in conflict-affected regions. The failure of US efforts to stabilize and rebuild South Vietnam highlighted the challenges of imposing political stability and social order in societies torn apart by war and internal strife.

- Subsequent interventions in places like Somalia, Bosnia, and Kosovo grappled with similar dilemmas and trade-offs, as policymakers and military leaders sought to balance humanitarian imperatives with strategic interests and political constraints. The Vietnam War served as a cautionary tale for the risks and limitations of external intervention in complex and volatile environments.

In conclusion, Chapter 14 reflects on the enduring lessons of the Vietnam War for US foreign policy and military strategy, as well as its impact on subsequent conflicts and interventions. From the reevaluation of limited war doctrine and counterinsurgency strategy to the challenges of civil-military relations and public opinion, the Vietnam War continues to shape debates and decisions about the use of force and the conduct of warfare in the contemporary world. By learning from the mistakes and experiences of the past, policymakers, military leaders, and society as a whole can strive to build a more peaceful, just, and secure future.

Chapter 15: Conclusion

The Vietnam War remains one of the most complex, controversial, and consequential conflicts in modern history. As we conclude our exploration of this multifaceted and deeply impactful chapter, Chapter 15 provides a summation of key themes and insights from the Vietnam War, along with final thoughts on its enduring significance and relevance in contemporary times.

Summation of Key Themes and Insights

1. Human Cost of War:
   - The Vietnam War exacted a devastating toll in terms of human lives, with millions of Vietnamese civilians and soldiers, as well as tens of thousands of American troops, losing their lives in the conflict. The war left deep scars on Vietnamese society and the American psyche, shaping cultural attitudes and political perceptions for generations to come.
   2. Failure of Military Interventionism:
   - The Vietnam War exposed the limitations and pitfalls of military interventionism as a tool of foreign policy, highlighting the challenges of waging war against determined and resilient adversaries in unfamiliar and hostile environments. The conflict shattered the myth of American invincibility and undermined public confidence in the government's ability to pursue military solutions to complex political problems.
   3. Lessons of Counterinsurgency:
   - The Vietnam War underscored the importance of developing effective counterinsurgency strategies to combat irregular warfare and insurgent movements. The failure of US forces to adequately address the underlying political, economic, and social grievances that fueled the communist insurgency in Vietnam highlighted the need for a comprehensive approach to counterinsurgency.
   4. Impact on Civil-Military Relations:

- The Vietnam War strained civil-military relations in the United States, exposing tensions and divisions between civilian policymakers and military leaders over strategy, objectives, and the conduct of the war. The erosion of trust and confidence between political and military leaders contributed to the breakdown of decision-making processes and hindered effective coordination and execution of military operations.

5. Legacy of Trauma and Healing:

- The Vietnam War left deep psychological scars on those who lived through it, both in Vietnam and the United States. Veterans of the war experienced high rates of post-traumatic stress disorder (PTSD), depression, and substance abuse, with many struggling to reintegrate into civilian life after returning home. Efforts to address the trauma of war and promote healing and reconciliation remain ongoing in both countries.

Final Thoughts on Enduring Significance and Relevance

The Vietnam War continues to resonate deeply in contemporary times, serving as a cautionary tale and a source of enduring lessons for policymakers, military leaders, and society as a whole. Its legacy looms large in debates and decisions about war, peace, and the use of force in the contemporary world.

1. Moral and Ethical Considerations:

- The Vietnam War raised important moral and ethical questions about the nature and conduct of warfare, the responsibility of governments to protect civilian populations, and the imperative of upholding human rights and humanitarian principles in times of conflict. These considerations remain central to contemporary debates about the ethics of military intervention and the responsibilities of states in the international system.

2. Lessons for US Foreign Policy:

- The Vietnam War has left a lasting imprint on US foreign policy, influencing attitudes and approaches towards military interventionism, nation-building, and diplomacy. Policymakers and military leaders continue to grapple with the lessons of Vietnam as they confront new challenges and crises on the global stage, seeking to avoid the mistakes and pitfalls of the past while adapting to the complexities of the present.

3. Pursuit of Peace and Reconciliation:

- Perhaps the most enduring legacy of the Vietnam War is its reminder of the human cost of war and the imperative of pursuing peace and reconciliation in the aftermath of conflict. The war's legacy of trauma and division serves as a poignant reminder of the need for empathy, understanding, and forgiveness in building a more peaceful and just world for future generations.

In conclusion, the Vietnam War stands as a testament to the complexity and tragedy of armed conflict, as well as the resilience and capacity for healing and reconciliation in its aftermath. By reflecting on the key themes and insights from the war and its enduring significance and relevance in contemporary times, we honor the memory of those who served and sacrificed and reaffirm our commitment to learning from the past in order to build a better future. As we strive to navigate the challenges of the present and shape the course of history, let us heed the lessons of Vietnam and work towards a world of peace, justice, and mutual respect.

Don't miss out!

Visit the website below and you can sign up to receive emails whenever Michael Johnson publishes a new book. There's no charge and no obligation.

https://books2read.com/r/B-A-OREFB-JHXZC

BOOKS 2 READ

Connecting independent readers to independent writers.

Did you love *The Vietnam War*? Then you should read *World War II*[1] by Michael Johnson!

[2]

"World War II: America's Role in the Global Conflict" chronicles the pivotal moments that defined America's involvement in the greatest conflict of the 20th century. From the seeds of conflict to the enduring legacy, delve into the chapters that shaped history, from America's initial stance of isolationism to its transformation into a global superpower. Experience the courage and sacrifice of those who fought on the front lines and the resilience of those who endured on the home front. This book is a testament to the indomitable spirit of the American people and their enduring legacy in shaping the world we live in today.

---

1. https://books2read.com/u/3k9aa8

2. https://books2read.com/u/3k9aa8

About the Author

Michael Johnson is a distinguished historian specializing in American history. With a degree in History from Harvard University, Johnson's work delves into pivotal moments, figures, and themes shaping the United States. He has authored numerous acclaimed books, offering insightful perspectives and engaging narratives. Johnson's commitment to meticulous scholarship and compelling storytelling has earned him widespread acclaim in the field. Passionate about sharing his expertise, he frequently engages in lectures and public events to foster a deeper appreciation for America's past.